OUR PLANET

Swamps

SHEILA GORE

Troll Associates

5539

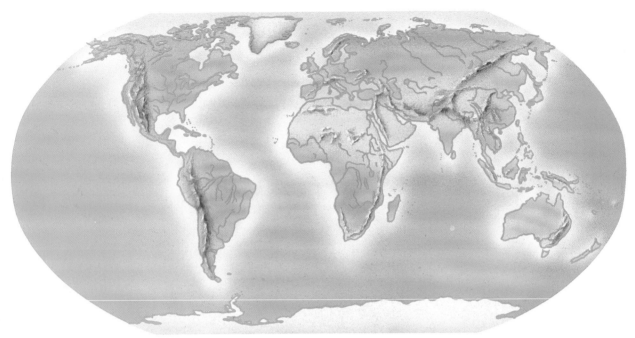

Library of Congress Cataloging-in-Publication Data

Gore, Sheila.
    Swamps / by Sheila Gore; illustrated by Robert Burns...[et
.al.].
       p.   cm.—(Our planet)
    Summary: Examines swamps, marshes, and other kinds of wetlands,
the kinds of life they support, and how they interact with the
environment surrounding them.
    ISBN 0-8167-2755-4 (lib. bdg.)   ISBN 0-8167-2756-2 (pbk.)
    1. Wetlands—Juvenile literature.   2. Swamps—Juvenile literature.
[1. Wetlands. 2. Wetland ecology. 3. Ecology.] I. Burns, Robert,
ill. II. Title. III. Series.
QH87.3.G67   1993
574.5 '26325—dc20   91-45081

Published by Troll Associates

Edited by Neil Morris and Kate Woodhouse

Design by Sally Boothroyd

Picture research by Jan Croot

Printed in the United States of America, bound in Mexico.

10 9 8 7 6 5 4 3 2 1

Illustrators
Robert Burns: 4
Martin Camm: 17, 18
Chris Forsey: 6-7, 8-9, 10
David McAllister: 23
David More: 15, 20, 27

Picture credits
FLPA: Leo Batten: 11
FLPA: M. Nimmo: 6
GSF Picture Library: 8-9, 9, 12, 12-13, 15, 20,
   22-23, 30
Hutchison Library: 25
NHPA: Anthony Bannister: 19
NHPA: L. Campbell: 20-21
NHPA: James J. Carmichael: 28-29
NHPA: Stephen Dalton: 16-17
NHPA: E. A. Janes: 4-5, 24
NHPA: G. E. Schmida: 16
NHPA: Martin Strange: 28
NHPA: Roger Tideman: 31
Paul C. Pet: 13
Silkeborg Museum: 14
Spectrum: cover
Survival Anglia: Jeff Foott: 1
Survival Anglia: Dieter and Mary Plage: 31
Survival Anglia: Vivek R. Sinha: 18
ZEFA: 26, 27

Cover photo:
Everglades National Park, Florida

Title page:
Mangrove swamps in Florida

CONTENTS

What is a wetland?

Wetland is the name given to any area of land with water-logged soil. Such areas have other, more specific, names, but the main types are swamps, marshes, fens, and bogs. There are no precise definitions for these terms, and what is called a bog in one part of the world might be called a moor somewhere else. *Taiga* is the Russian name for marshy pine forests, and *fen* is an Old Norse word for land that is often covered with water.

The level of water in the ground is called the water table. In some places it is well below ground, and the soil is dry. In others it is near, at, or above ground level, which creates the conditions for a wetland. The water table may go up or down. In winter and spring when there has been more rain, or melted snow has come down from nearby mountains, the water table tends to be higher.

Wetlands are mostly low-lying and featureless, but they are among the most productive environments in the world. They are often rich in minerals, support a wide variety of wildlife, and can be natural flood controls.

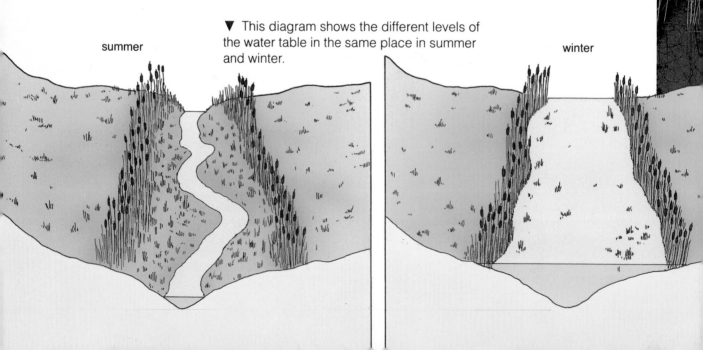

▼ This diagram shows the different levels of the water table in the same place in summer and winter.

summer

winter

▲ In wetlands, land and water mingle. If plants are not disturbed they build up into islands. Mosses are the first to grow, trapping water and mud. Sometimes, mosses and other plants make a platform where shrubs and trees can grow.

Most people define a swamp as an area that is permanently wet, but where trees and shrubs grow. A marsh is similar, but its plants tend to be grasses. A bog has small amounts of shallow water visible, and its surface is wet, spongy, and often covered with moss.

5

Ancient wetlands

Swamps were the earliest environment to support land life on Earth. The first animals and plants adapted to live partly on land and partly in the water. *Ichthyostega* is the earliest known amphibian. It lived about 350 million years ago. It probably laid its eggs in water, but was able to breathe air, just as present-day amphibians do. The first plants were like modern ferns and mosses. They were very small, and their leaves could survive out of water. But to reproduce, their seeds had to travel through water.

From these beginnings, life in the swamps flourished. Between 300 and 200 million years ago, much of North America and Europe was covered with dense forests growing in swamps. Huge tree ferns and giant horsetails towered up to 100 feet (30 meters) over the forests. There were amphibians, insects, and other invertebrates living among the trees.

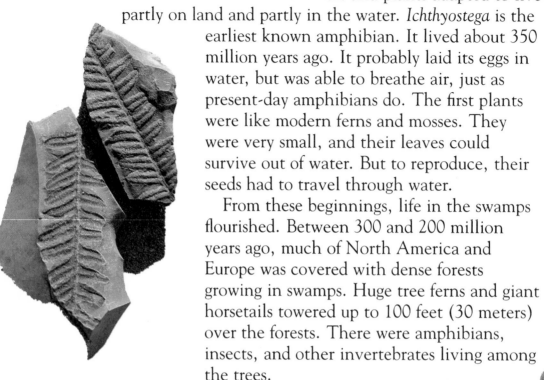

▲ These rocks have the fossil imprints of ferns that grew millions of years ago in vast swamps.

These ancient wetland forests are sometimes called coal forests. As the trees died, they fell down and over many years formed a thick layer of vegetation. This layer was compressed and fossilized to become the coal deposits that are mined today.

Our knowledge of these ancient wetlands comes from the fossils found in the smooth black mud between coal deposits and in other rocks. Fossils are rarely found in coal itself.

▼ Much of Europe and North America 200 to 300 million years ago was covered with coal forests like this one.

Coastal wetlands

Along some sheltered coastlines, sediments accumulate that enable plants to grow and become established. The roots of these plants trap more sediment, and gradually a coastal wetland is created. There are two broad types of coastal wetlands: mangrove swamps in the tropics and salt marshes in cooler climates.

Survival for plants growing between the sea and the land is hard. The plants need to be able to tolerate the low levels of oxygen found in many wetlands, as well as the salty seawater and the regular wetting and drying caused by tides. One feature of these wetlands is the plants that grow in bands, or zones, each adapted to different levels of saltiness of the water. The saltiest zones are inland from the high-tide mark, where seawater evaporates regularly and leaves salt in the topsoil.

Mangrove swamps are named for the trees that grow in them. The trees are specially adapted to coastal wetlands. They all have an underground system of anchor roots. Above the mud of the wetland, some mangroves have large, curving roots like stilts, and others have upright aerial roots. Both these types of roots have many small pores that allow air, but not water, to pass through them. In this way they can survive in what appears to be an impossible environment.

Salt marshes in temperate parts of the world do not have such distinctive trees. But they have many different kinds of plants and wildlife, depending on the saltiness of the water and the extent of flooding by the sea.

▶ The trees in this mangrove swamp have the stilt type of roots, allowing them to grow above the level of the water. They form a dense barrier which is difficult to penetrate.

8

► It is easy to lose your way in this flat, featureless landscape. The maze of water weaves around with no apparent direction. Plants, like the sea lavender in this picture, can stretch for miles. There are wetlands like this along many coastlines in temperate parts of the world.

Lake marshes

Around the edge of most lakes, land merges gradually with water to create wetland. These areas are usually thick with different types of reeds. They have their roots and some of their leaves and stems underwater, but stand 3 feet (one meter) or more out of the water.

The Everglades in southern Florida are one of the biggest and most famous lake-marsh areas. You can boat between the vast expanses of sawgrass and look for tiny frogs, snapping turtles, alligators, or colonies of birds, such as egrets or herons. Some of the animals in the Everglades are becoming rare. One is the *anhinga*, or snakebird, which kills and catches fish by spearing them with its sharp beak.

Tiny algae and water plants grow in the shallow water of lake marshes. These provide food for water fleas, dragonflies, damselflies, and other insects. The insects are eaten by newts, frogs, and toads, which in turn feed the birds. This food chain is vital to the survival of lake marshes. If even one link in the chain is polluted or destroyed, the whole environment is threatened.

At first a lake marsh may seem rather dull, but when you look more closely, there is a huge range of plants and insects that are unique to that environment.

► Lush tropical vegetation fringes the lake wetlands of Florida. Sediment is trapped between the roots of the plants, which allows other plants to establish themselves.

▼ This picture shows a simple type of food chain that exists in many lake marshes.

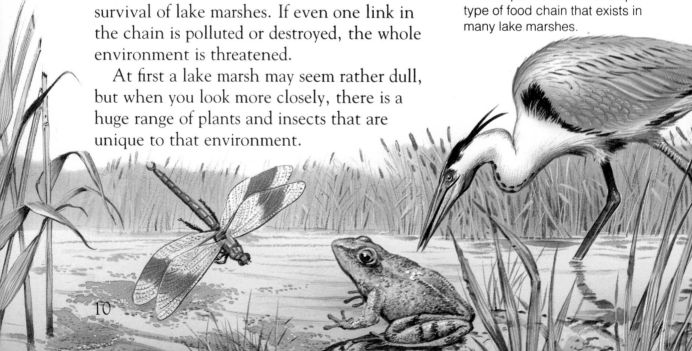

River marshes

On higher ground, river water is usually moving fast. This means that the river keeps within its banks, and there is a distinct border between wet and dry. In addition, sediment is carried down by the river and does not accumulate. On lower reaches, the river moves across a flatter landscape, and the water slows down, often meandering across a flood plain. This is where river wetlands, or marshes, develop. These wetlands are not normally stagnant or lacking in oxygen, because fresh water is always being brought down the river. This encourages a lush and varied plant life.

◀ This weaverbird lives in the Okavango Delta in Botswana. It needs to lay its eggs and allow them to hatch in a safe place.
▼ The weaverbird snips off thin strands of reed and weaves them together to make a nest. The nest is completely enclosed around a reed with a tube-like entrance at its base.

▶ Not all wetlands are natural. This wetland was created in order to cultivate rice, which is planted by hand in the muddy waters of the paddy field. Originally wild rice grew in the freshwater wetlands of lakes.

When a river reaches the sea, it often forms a delta, which creates its own unique wetland. The Ganges Delta in Bangladesh, for example, is flooded by rich, fertile soil, which is essential for growing rice. Rice is one of the most important wetland plants.

Both freshwater and saltwater marshes are particularly important as breeding and feeding grounds for birds. Bird watching on a marsh can be very rewarding. There is usually a huge variety of birds to see. Some are permanent residents, and others are resting from a long migration.

Highland bogs

Bogs are usually on higher ground, where there is a lot of rain and water cannot drain away easily. Bogs often formed in lakes that were created by glaciers in the ice ages. Water-loving moss, such as *sphagnum*, spreads quickly across wetlands, draining open stretches of water. Dead and decaying matter builds up underneath the moss to form a mat across the water, creating a dangerous, quivering surface that looks solid until you step on it. Over the years, the moss builds up to form a peat bog, which will then support more substantial plant life, such as trees. Eventually, the wetland could dry up completely with such thirsty plant life.

Peat bogs are famous for their preserving qualities. Danish peat cutters discovered an almost perfectly preserved human body in the Tollund bog of Jutland. Tollund man retained his facial expression, hair, and a leather hat for almost 2,000 years.

◀ Tollund man looks much less than 2,000 years old! There is very little oxygen in peat so almost nothing lives in it. This means that plants and animals, and in this case people, decay extremely slowly.

▶ The Arctic fox looks very different from foxes that live in temperate climates. It is adapted to living in the tundra. Its thick, white fur makes it hard to see in the snow and its short snout and small ears reduce the risk of frostbite.

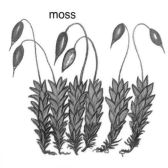
moss

In the Arctic, the tundra is frozen for most of the year. In spring, the top layers of soil thaw, but deeper layers stay frozen and prevent the water from draining away. These temporary soggy conditions create the tundra wetlands where animals such as caribou feed off the succulent small shrubs and plants that grow quickly in the summer months.

Animals of the wetlands

The wetlands provide an ideal habitat for many species of insects. Many of these insects spend only the early stages of their lives in the water. For example, dragonfly young breathe underwater through gills and eat other insects and tadpoles by extending their lower lips and grasping their prey. They spend about a year underwater, then climb a reed or rock and shed their skins to fly off as dragonflies.

Mosquitoes also flourish in wetlands. The females are bloodsuckers and need a meal before they lay their eggs. Each female plunges its *proboscis*, or feeding tube, into animals or humans to suck blood. At the same time, she pumps saliva into the victim to prevent the blood from clotting immediately. Serious diseases such as malaria and yellow fever can be carried by mosquitoes and given to humans in this way. Because of this, wetlands can be an unhealthy environment for people.

▲ This water snake slithers through the water by flexing its body from side to side.

◄ A terrapin's webbed feet and streamlined body mean it can walk on land and swim well. Its long neck allows the terrapin to see above water while its body is hidden.

marsh frog

Amphibians are common in wetlands, which are the ideal habitat for animals that need both water and dry land. It's easy to see a frog near a marsh, and at night it can be quite noisy, with frogs and toads calling to each other. Reptiles are also widespread, but mainly in the warmer parts of the world. Mangrove swamps are home to crocodiles, turtles, and snakes, which slither and slip between the mangrove roots searching for food.

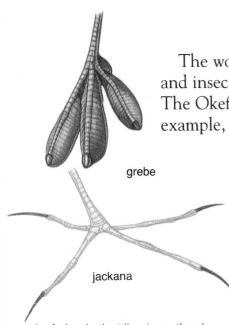

grebe

jackana

▲ Animals that live in wetlands tend to have splayed feet that make walking easier.

The wonderful opportunities for feeding on plants and insects mean that birds are attracted to wetlands. The Okefenokee Swamp in the United States, for example, is home to over 200 species of birds. Many birds are specially adapted to living on marshland. Some have delicate, widespread toes, and others, such as storks, herons, and flamingoes, have long, spindly legs so they can wade through shallow water in search of food. The marsh plants can act as shelter and camouflage. The reed warbler builds a cup-shaped nest suspended between supporting reed stems. The bittern has speckled feathers, but when it points its bill upwards and stands still, it blends in with the surrounding reeds.

◄ This barasingha is knee-deep in water plants. It is wading through a shallow lake and grazing on the lush vegetation. Its broad hooves and long legs make wading quite easy.

► These squabbling marabou storks in the Kruger National Park in South Africa have long, thin toes that spread wide to keep them from sinking into the waterlogged mud. They use their pointed, powerful beaks to catch fish in the water around them.

Mammals are also adapted to living in wetlands. The *sitatunga*, a type of antelope, and swamp deer have broad hooves for walking on soggy ground. The marsh rabbit can escape any enemies by swimming away! Many marshes have a variety of small mammals, such as the muskrat, which can stay underwater for up to twelve minutes. Muskrats eat the roots of water plants, but they also catch clams, and sometimes fish.

Plants of the wetlands

Plants growing in swamps, marshes, or bogs have to adapt to the special conditions of these environments. Trees and bushes tend to grow well in swamps, where the soil is reasonably fertile and the ground not too wet.

River marshes have water plants and plants that are rooted in water but grow in the air above. It is in the saltwater marshes, particularly, that plants have to adapt.

sundew

▶ Wetlands often lack nitrogen, which is vital for healthy plant growth. Carnivorous plants make up for this by trapping insects and absorbing nitrogen from them.

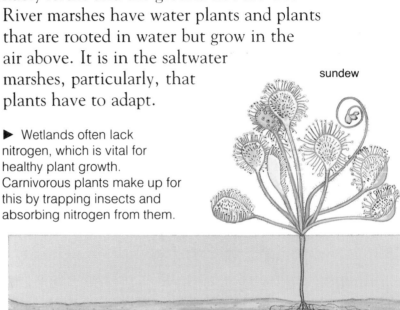

▲ This ant is wrapped up and trapped in the tentacles of the sundew plant.

Plants that grow in soil covered by salt water are called *halophytes*. Their survival depends on being able to overcome the salt around them. Some eliminate salt through their leaves. Others filter the salty water, and any salt that does enter the plant is stored in succulent leaves. Some of these plants, like glasswort, look like desert plants.

The poor soil of some bogs lacks the nitrogen vital for plant growth. For this reason, carnivorous, or animal-eating, plants flourish in bogs, because they can get all the nitrogen they need from the insects they catch. For example, the bladderwort has no roots. It grows in water with bladder-like leaves that float just below the surface. Tiny hairs on each bladder can trigger a trap door, so that a passing flea that touches the hairs is sucked in and the trap door closes behind it.

▼ Migrating birds such as these Brent geese rely on the coastal grassy wetlands for food. It looks very bare, but there is plenty for these birds to eat.

People of the wetlands

Swamps, marshes, and bogs are usually difficult places for people to live in. However, people have lived in some of the wetlands of the world. For centuries, nomadic Marsh Arabs of Iraq lived on the permanent marshland between the Euphrates and Tigris rivers. The marsh is made up of lagoons and giant reeds. The reeds, which grow up to 20 feet (6 meters) high, were used to build artificial islands in the lagoons. The Arabs also used reeds to make houses.

Since marshes are usually hard to get to, they have been used as places of refuge. For example, the Seminole Indians of the southeastern United States lived in the Everglades area of Florida to escape their enemies. They now live on a reservation area in the Everglades National Park.

Some of the people of Thailand have lived in houses on stilts for hundreds of years. They live above the marshwaters and travel everywhere by boat. People flood the marshes so they can grow rice. They can also fish in the nearby river.

◀ People living beside the Amazon have built houses on stilts rather than cutting deep into the forest to build on dry land. Here they can fish and use the river water.

▼ The Marsh Arabs of Iraq used giant wetland reeds to build their houses. They kept buffalo that grazed on the water plants.

Wetlands in danger

People have affected the marshes and bogs of the world for many years, but never more so than now. The fens of eastern England were created by the over-digging of peat by the Romans two thousand years ago. Today, the mechanical digging of peat is threatening their future. Some people think there will be no more peat in ten years' time if this continues.

All over the world wetlands are being drained. More than half of the original wetlands in the United States have been drained to provide rich agricultural land. In Africa, there are plans to drain the huge Okavango Swamps in Botswana for mining and agriculture.

▼ Water from the surrounding fields is draining into this ditch. Sometimes chemicals used on the fields also drain into the ditch. This could damage plants and wildlife taking water from the ditch.

► This machine is dredging out a drainage canal running between fields in the Sudan. Many natural wetland areas are claimed for agricultural land in this way.

The Jonglei Canal in the Sudan is being built to divert water from the Sudd Swamp to Egypt and northern Sudan. This will reduce the grassland of the flood plain and disrupt farming and animals in the area.

Sometimes it is the drainage of the tributaries, or feeder rivers, that can cause the wetlands to dry out. One of the best-known examples of this is the Aswan High Dam in Egypt. This dam was opened in 1968 to prevent the seasonal flooding of the Nile River. The farmers now have to use expensive and damaging chemicals, instead of the rich silt that came from flooding, to fertilize their crops. In addition, the sardine-fishing industry of the Nile Delta has declined dramatically, and sea salt once washed back by the river is now reaching further inland. This has made some soil too salty to cultivate.

▲ A satellite photograph of the Nile Delta, showing its triangular shape.

◄ Vast dams like the Aswan in Egypt provide power to generate electricity and control the flow of water in the arid regions of North Africa. But they also disrupt the natural action of the river.

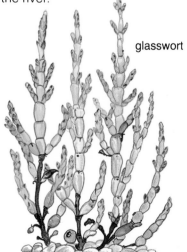

glasswort

Many waterways are now used for vacation boats. But too many people and too many motorboats can easily upset the plants and wildlife of any wetland. Swamps and marshes are best suited to a few people using them, traveling by canoe or rowboat.

Scientists have discovered that some wetland plants and their bacteria can naturally filter some metal pollutants out of water. This could prevent fish from taking in toxic substances and poisoning the food chain. This would be a worthwhile scientific use of wetlands and their plants.

27

The future

From lush tropical mangrove swamps to vast moorland, wetlands support a spectacular range of life. They sustain huge flocks of migrating birds in their journey across continents. Coal, one of the most valuable fuels for the world's industrial development, was formed in swamps, and yet we often ignore or destroy this environment.

▲ This wetland in Sarawak has been made a national park that people can visit and study.

Fortunately, many people now realize the value of wetlands, and many countries have made them national parks or conservation areas. In 1971, an international organization was set up to help protect wetlands all over the world. So far it has saved over 77,000 square miles (200,000 square kilometers) of wetlands.

Wetlands are not poor, useless habitats that need to be "improved." Like any special habitat, they play a part in the balance of nature, and their survival is important. Very often small areas of marsh can be preserved, perhaps near where you live. This might mean that some marsh flowers, and perhaps some birds and insects, will be able to continue living there. It is not just the large wetlands of the world that need to be protected. Small swamps and marshes are important, too.

► Fisheating Creek in Florida. Canoeing is one of the best ways of exploring the wetlands in this part of Florida.

Fact file

Extent of wetlands
It is estimated that there are about 3,280,000 square miles (8,500,000 square kilometers) of wetlands worldwide.

Preservation of wetlands
The Convention of Wetlands is of international importance, especially since Wildfowl Habitats was set up in 1971. So far, it has saved around 77,000 square miles (200,000 square kilometers) of wetlands from being drained and developed. Swamps and marshes are home to many rare species of fish, salamanders, frogs, and birds. These animals would soon disappear if the wetlands were destroyed.

Valuable coastal edges
It is estimated that around two-thirds of the U.S.'s coastal fish and shellfish rely on wetlands for food, spawning grounds, and nurseries. European wetlands also support many of the fish of its seas.

Water storage
Wetlands have an important part to play in the storage of water. A 6-inch (15-centimeter) rise in a 10-acre (4-hectare) marsh stores more than 1.5 million gallons (6.8 million liters) of water. It would be tempting to put all this water to other uses, but this would mean the end of the wetlands.

Peat digging
Peat has been dug by hand for centuries in northern Europe. The peat is laid out to dry in rows and then collected and stored for the winter fires. Small-scale digging like this presents little danger to the peat bog, but in recent years mechanical diggers have gouged out massive amounts of peat to sell for garden centers.

Rice growing
Vast terraces of flooded paddy fields are used to grow rice. Mud is banked up to create terraces and water is pumped or channeled to the fields.

▼ Terraced rice fields in Indonesia

▲ Drying peat in Scotland

Supporting people

Many plant crops started as wetland plants—for example, rice, sago palm, and oil palm. Long ago, North Americans harvested rice from wetlands on the shores of the Great Lakes between the United States and Canada.

Largest swamp

The largest swamp in the world is in the Ukraine. The basin of the Pripyat River, north of Kiev, is estimated to cover 18,125 square miles (47,125 square kilometers).

Water temperatures

The temperature of water in swamps can vary by as much as 27°F (15° C) in one day. Swamp water often looks brown because of the acids given off by decaying vegetation. Sunlight cannot reach more than about 3 feet (1 meter) into swamp water.

Mudskippers

Mudskippers live in mangrove swamps. They are fish but are able to survive for a short time out of water. They prop themselves up on their strong front flippers and skip across the mud. Some of them have suckers that enable them to stick to the roots of mangrove trees.

Flood control

River swamps also act as flood control. They absorb and store large amounts of water, which they release gradually, so that any flood is slowed and reduced.

▼ Mudskippers

Index